# Missouri
## The Show-Me State

Marcia Amidon Lusted

PowerKiDS press™
New York

Published in 2010 by The Rosen Publishing Group, Inc.
29 East 21st Street, New York, NY 10010

First Edition

Editor: Nicole Pristash
Book Design: Greg Tucker
Layout Design: Julio Gil
Photo Researcher: Jessica Gerweck

Photo Credits: Cover © Walter Bibikow/JAI/Corbis; p. 5 John Elk III/Getty Images; p. 7 © David David Gallery/SuperStock; p. 9 Hulton Archive/Getty Images; p. 11 Phil Schermeister/Getty Images; p. 13 © www.iStockphoto.com/Jakub Pavlinec; p. 15 © Bill Barksdale/age fotostock; pp. 17, 22 (flag, bird, bee) Shutterstock.com; p. 19 Jason Todd/Getty Images; p. 22 (tree) © www.iStockphoto.com/Aimin Tang; p. 22 (mule) © www.iStockphoto.com/Michael Klenetsky; p. 22 (Harry S. Truman) Stock Montage/Getty Images; p. 22 (Maya Angelou) WireImage/Getty Images; p. 22 (Jamie McMurray) Geoff Burke/Getty Images.

Library of Congress Cataloging-in-Publication Data

Lusted, Marcia Amidon.
  Missouri : the Show-Me State / Marcia Amidon Lusted. — 1st ed.
      p. cm. — (Our amazing states)
  Includes index.
  ISBN 978-1-4358-9351-1 (library binding) — ISBN 978-1-4358-9796-0 (pbk.) — ISBN 978-1-4358-9797-7 (6-pack)
  1. Missouri—Juvenile literature. I. Title.
  F466.3.L87 2010
  977.8—dc22
                                      2009030779

Manufactured in the United States of America

CPSIA Compliance Information: Batch #WW10PK: For Further Information contact Rosen Publishing, New York, New York at 1-800-237-9932

# Contents

# Gateway to the West

There is a state in which you can ride to the top of the Gateway **Arch**, eat tasty barbecue, and take a boat ride on the Mississippi River. Which state is this? It is Missouri! Missouri played a big part in the westward **expansion** of the United States. In the 1800s, many **pioneer** trails, railroads, and river journeys started there. Thousands of pioneers passed through the state on their way west.

Missouri's nickname is the Show-Me State. The name comes from a Missouri congressman, Willard Duncan Vandiver. He said in a speech in 1899 that fancy language did not satisfy him. "I am from Missouri," he said. "You have got to show me." The name is often used to describe how people who live in Missouri are not easily swayed.

This is one of the many riverboats that travel along the Mississippi River in Missouri. Riding a riverboat is a great way to see the sights of Missouri.

# Missouri's Past

People have lived in Missouri as far back as 12,000 BC. The first European **explorers** came in the 1670s. Famous explorers Meriwether Lewis and William Clark came through the area in 1804 as they explored the West.

In 1818, Missouri wanted to join the United States as a slave state. At that time, there was an equal number of free states and slave states. If Missouri became a slave state, it would upset this balance. In 1820, the Missouri **Compromise** was passed. It allowed Missouri to join the United States as a slave state because Maine would join as a free state. The compromise also said that all states north of Missouri would be free states. Those south of and including Missouri would be slave states.

This painting shows Lewis and Clark during their exploration of the western states. In 1804, Lewis and Clark spent around a month in Missouri.

# An Important Case

In the 1830s, a slave from Missouri named Dred Scott went to live in free states and territories with his owner. After moving back to Missouri, Scott's owner died. Scott then went to court. He stated that because he had lived in free areas, he should be free. In 1857, the **Supreme Court** ruled that slaves could never be U.S. citizens. Therefore, they could not go to court. It also ruled that the Missouri Compromise was **unconstitutional**. Since slaves were property, the government could not ban people from owning them.

The country was split on whether slavery should be allowed, and disagreements would soon lead to the **Civil War**. Missouri played a big part in one of U.S. history's most important events.

After losing his case in court, Dred Scott was freed by his owner's sons. Sadly, he died nine months later.

Missouri is located in the midwestern part of the United States. Because it is surrounded by eight other states, it is sometimes called the most neighborly state in the country. Missouri has rolling hills as well as steep mountains and flat plains. The Missouri River winds through the center of the state, and the Mississippi River forms the eastern border.

All parts of Missouri have the same kind of weather. Summers can be hot, and in the winter, it gets cold enough to snow. Thunderstorms and **tornadoes** happen often there, bringing dangerous winds. There are sometimes earthquakes in Missouri, too. An earthquake in 1811 was so strong that parts of the Mississippi River flowed backward for a short time!

Barges, such as the one shown here, can often be seen traveling on the Mississippi River. Barges are flat-bottomed boats that are used to move heavy goods.

# Missouri's Wildlife

Missouri is home to many plants, such as pale purple coneflowers, red Indian paintbrush, and blue wild indigo. Trees, such as oak, birch, dogwood, and tulip, grow in the state as well.

Thousands of different types of animals live in Missouri. Some of the more familiar animals that you may see in the state are beavers, bobcats, opossums, and black bears. Bats and mountain lions live there, too. Missouri's state animal is the Missouri mule. It may seem like an odd choice for the state animal, but the mule was chosen for a good reason. In the 1800s, mules were used to pull the wagons of pioneers who were going west. The mule is known for being very strong and very **stubborn**!

Mules can carry around 20 percent of their body weight. This means that an 800-pound (363 kg) mule can carry a load that is around 160 pounds (73 kg).

# Farms and Fighter Jets

Many of the things that you eat every day may have come from Missouri. The state has the second-highest number of farms in the country. These farms grow everything from soybeans and corn to cotton and potatoes. Missouri farmers also raise cows, hogs, and chickens.

Missouri is more than just farms, though. The birthday card that you got on your birthday may have come from Hallmark Cards, in Kansas City. The Boeing Company in St. Louis builds fighter jets for the military. Is there a new sidewalk being built in your town? The **cement** may have come from a limestone **quarry** in Missouri! One of Missouri's biggest businesses is taking care of all the **tourists** who visit every year.

This farmer in Missouri is checking his corn crop. In 2007, there were more than 3 million acres (1.2 million ha) of cornfields in the state.

# Exploring Missouri

Most capital cities in the United States were already cities before they became state capitals. However, in the 1820s, Jefferson City was built just to be Missouri's capital city. Daniel Morgan Boone, whose father was the famous **frontiersman** Daniel Boone, planned the city. Today, there are many interesting things to do in Jefferson City. You can visit the Missouri State Museum or walk through Jefferson Landing, where settlers first came into the city.

If you like barbecue, then Kansas City may be the place for you. Kansas City, in western Missouri, is famous for its barbecue. Restaurants there cook all sorts of meats with special sauces. Kansas City is sometimes called the world's barbecue capital. It has more than 100 barbecue restaurants!

Kansas City, shown here, is the most populated city in Missouri. About 440,000 people live there.

One of Missouri's most famous places is the Gateway Arch, in St. Louis. The arch is made of stainless steel, and it is as tall as a 63-story building. It is the tallest monument in the United States. The arch took 900 tons (816 t) of steel to build. Finished in 1965, it honors Missouri's history as the gateway to the West.

If you go to St. Louis, you can visit the top of the Gateway Arch. More than a million visitors do this every year. They ride in special cars inside the arch that carry them to a deck at the top. From there, visitors can see things that are 30 miles (48 km) away. On a windy day, the arch can sway back and forth almost 1 inch (2.5 cm)!

The Gateway Arch is 630 feet (192 m) tall. That is more than twice the height of the Statue of Liberty!

# Come to Missouri!

If you ever visit Missouri, there are lots of things to do. Visitors can go to the Hollywood Wax Museum, in Branson, to see wax **sculptures** of famous people. At Elephant Rocks State Park, in southeastern Missouri, you can see large rocks that look like elephants. Visitors can celebrate National Tom Sawyer Days, in Hannibal, where *Tom Sawyer* author Mark Twain lived as a boy. If you visit St. Louis, you can watch a hot-air balloon race and cheer for the St. Louis Cardinals at Busch Stadium. Many people simply enjoy nature in one of Missouri's national forests.

Missouri is an amazing state. Whether you like history, food, or nature, Missouri is the place for you!

# Glossary

**arch** (AHRCH)  A frame that curves at the top and makes an opening.

**cement** (sih-MENT)  A mix of water, sand, and rock that hardens and is often used for building.

**Civil War** (SIH-vul WOR)  The war fought between the Northern and the Southern states of America from 1861 to 1865.

**compromise** (KOM-pruh-myz)  Something given up to reach an agreement.

**expansion** (ek-SPAN-shun)  The widening or opening of an area.

**explorers** (ek-SPLOR-erz)  People who travel and look for new land.

**frontiersman** (frun-TEERZ-man)  A man who lives and works in an unsettled area.

**pioneer** (py-uh-NEER)  A person who settles in a new area.

**quarry** (KWOR-ee)  A large hole, dug in the ground, from which stone is taken.

**sculptures** (SKULP-cherz)  Figures that are shaped or formed.

**stubborn** (STUH-burn)  Wanting to have one's own way.

**Supreme Court** (suh-PREEM KORT)  The highest court in the United States.

**tornadoes** (tawr-NAY-dohz)  Storms with funnel-shaped clouds that produce strong, spinning winds.

**tourists** (TUR-ists)  People visiting a place where they do not live.

**unconstitutional** (un-kon-stih-TOO-shuh-nul)  Going against the basic rules by which a country or a state is governed.

# Missouri State Symbols

State Tree
Flowering Dogwood

State Animal
Missouri Mule

State Flag

State Bird
Bluebird

State Insect
Honeybee

State Seal

## Famous People from Missouri

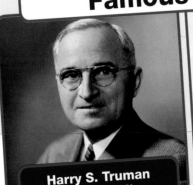

**Harry S. Truman**
(1884–1972)
Born in Lamar, MO
U.S. President

**Maya Angelou**
(1928– )
Born in St. Louis, MO
Poet

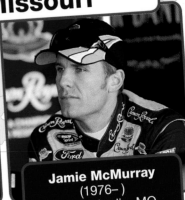

**Jamie McMurray**
(1976– )
Born in Joplin, MO
NASCAR driver

# Missouri State Map

## Legend

○ Major City

✪ Capital

〜 River

# Missouri State Facts

**Population:** About 5,596,678

**Area:** 69,697 square miles (180,514 sq km)

**Motto:** "Salus Populi Suprema Lex Esto" ("Let the welfare of the people be the supreme law")

**Song:** "Missouri Waltz," words by J. R. Shannon and music by John V. Eppel and Frederic Knight Logan

# Index

# Web Sites

Due to the changing nature of Internet links, PowerKids Press has developed an online list of Web sites related to the subject of this book. This site is updated regularly. Please use this link to access the list:

www.powerkidslinks.com/amst/mo/